Contents

Some words are shown in bold, **like this**. You can find out what they mean by looking in the Glossary.

Tora! Tora! Tora!

Total surprise

At dawn, one Sunday, Japan attacked the US naval base at Pearl Harbor, in Hawaii. Flying to the call sign *Tora! Tora! Tora!* (Tiger! Tiger! Tiger!), two waves of carrier-based planes severely damaged or destroyed 21 ships and over 300 aircraft, and caused 3500 **casualties**. The Japanese lost 29 aircraft, five midget submarines and 64 men. Japan's formal declaration of war only came after the attack started. To Americans this was not **aggression** – it was **treachery.**

Retreat from victory

The Japanese failed to hit three US aircraft-carriers out at sea. Not knowing the position of these ships, the Japanese feared a counter-attack. Rather than risk a third attack against Pearl Harbor's oil stores and repair facilities, the Japanese sailed home.

America united

Until Pearl Harbor was attacked many Americans wanted to stay out of the wars raging in Europe and Asia. Pearl Harbor enraged American opinion. President Franklin D. Roosevelt declared to Congress:

Of the 1400 crew of the USS *Arizona*, 1102 were killed. The wreck is now an official war grave. Most of the other ships that were sunk or damaged were repaired to fight again.

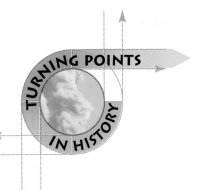

Pearl Harbor

The USA enters World War II

RICHARD TAMES

www.heinemann.co.uk
Visit our website to find out more information about **Heinemann Library** books.

To order:
☎ Phone 44 (0) 1865 888066
🗎 Send a fax to 44 (0) 1865 314091
💻 Visit the Heinemann Bookshop at www.heinemann.co.uk to browse our catalogue and order online.

First published in Great Britain by Heinemann Library, Halley Court, Jordan Hill, Oxford OX2 8EJ, a division of Reed Educational and Professional Publishing Ltd. Heinemann is a registered trademark of Reed Educational & Professional Publishing Limited.

OXFORD MELBOURNE AUCKLAND JOHANNESBURG BLANTYRE
GABORONE IBADAN PORTSMOUTH NH (USA) CHICAGO

Designed by Robert Sydenham, Ambassador Design, Bristol
Illustrations by Dewi Morris and Robert Sydenham, Ambassador Design, Bristol
Originated by Ambassador Litho Ltd
Printed in Hong Kong

ISBN 0 431 06917 4 (hardback)   ISBN 0 431 06924 7 (paperback)
05 04 03 02 01   05 04 03 02 01
10 9 8 7 6 5 4 3 2   10 9 8 7 6 5 4 3 2 1

British Library Cataloguing in Publication Data
Tames, Richard, 1946–
Pearl Harbor: the U.S. enters World War II. – (Turning points in history)
1. Pearl Harbor (Hawaii), Attack on, 1941 – Juvenile literature
I. Title
940.5'426

Acknowledgements
The Publishers would like to thank the following for permission to reproduce photographs:
Corbis: pp. 9, 14, 17, 20, (Bettman) pp. 4, 13, 19, 21, 23, (George Hall) p. 29, (Minnesota History) p. 16, (Museum of Flight), p. 15, (The Mariner's Museum), p. 11; Hulton Getty: pp. 5, 18, 24; Tames, Richard: pp. 6, 7, 10, 25, 27; Tony Stone Images: p. 26.

Cover photograph reproduced with permission of Corbis.

Our thanks to Christopher Gibb for his comments in the preparation of this book.

Every effort has been made to contact copyright holders of any material reproduced in this book. Any omissions will be rectified in subsequent printings if notice is given to the Publisher.

'Yesterday, December 7 1941 – a date that will live in **infamy** – the United States of America was suddenly and deliberately attacked by ... the Empire of Japan ... our people, our territory and our interests are in grave danger ... With confidence in our armed forces ... we will gain the inevitable triumph. So help us God.'

Sleeping giant

While his comrades celebrated, Admiral Yamamoto Isoroku, planner of the attack, warned grimly, 'I fear we have only awakened a sleeping giant and his reaction will be terrible.' Yamamoto, a former naval **attaché** in Washington, had strongly opposed war with America.

This newspaper appeared within 90 minutes of Japan's attack on Pearl Harbor, on the Hawaiian island of Oahu. The final death toll was much higher than that stated in the headlines.

EYEWITNESS

John Garcia, who was sixteen at the time, was a civilian engineer. He remembers the attack and the events that followed.

'I spent the day swimming ... I brought out I don't know how many bodies ... The following morning I went with my tools to the *West Virginia*. It had turned turtle, totally upside down ...

'About 300 men we cut out of there were still alive by the eighteenth day. It took two weeks to get all the fires out. ... they told me a shell had hit the house of my girl ... they said it was a Japanese bomb. Later we learned it was an American shell. She was killed ... getting ready for church.'

Opening up Japan

Japan meets the West – 1

Japan had no contact with western countries until Portuguese ships arrived in 1543. A century of trade followed, which brought in new technology, such as clocks and guns. From 1639 Japan closed off contact with the outside world, gaining security from intruders but falling behind in technology.

Japan meets the West – 2

War against Mexico (1846–48) brought California under American control. From there Americans wanted to trade with China. In 1853 the US Navy forced Japan – at gunpoint – to open up its seaports for American ships to buy food and water, for repair and for trade. Over the next half-century Japan imported western technology and institutions in order to transform itself into a modern industrial and military power.

In 1850 Yokohama was a tiny fishing village of wooden houses. By 1875 it had western-style stone buildings and Japan's first railway.

Enrich the country! Strengthen the army!

Unlike the government of its great neighbour, China, which tried to ignore western powers, Japan's leaders saw they represented both a threat and an opportunity. Japan adopted a western-style calendar, coinage, postal system and weights and measures. German instructors trained the new army. The British built the first railway, trained the navy and supplied its ships. American advisors reformed education and agriculture. By the 1890s Japan had its own steel-mills and shipyards and no longer needed foreign experts. To avoid becoming a **colony** of one of the expanding western empires, Japan became powerful enough to create an empire of its own.

Japan emerges

Victory over China in 1894–95 brought Japan rice-rich Taiwan as her first colony. In 1902 Britain became Japan's **ally**. This enabled Japan to defeat Russia for control of Korea in 1904–5 because Britain kept France, Russia's ally, out of the war. Japanese sea-power was decisive in both these victories. Successful wars made the armed forces popular and powerful in Japan itself.

The battleship *Mikasa*, Admiral Togo's flagship at the battle of Tsushima, off the coast of Japan, was built in England and launched in 1902.

THE RUSSO–JAPANESE WAR 1904–5

The Russo–Japanese war for Korea began with the Japanese navy trapping the Russian Pacific fleet in its base at Port Arthur in China. On land the two sides fought to a standstill. Meanwhile Russia's Baltic fleet sailed more than half-way round the world to join in. When it reached the Straits of Tsushima in May 1905 the Japanese fleet, under Admiral Togo, wiped it out completely within a matter of hours. After that Russia agreed to peace.

Expanding America westward

From east to west

Colonial America was settled from Britain by sea and prospered by seaborne trade. Quarrels over taxes on that trade led to the war for American independence. That war gave the USA its first navy. Americans then spread westward to control California by 1849. The USA then looked west to the Pacific and Asia for trade as well as east across the Atlantic to Europe.

An admiral's advice

In 1890, US Admiral A. T. Mahan wrote a book called *The Influence of Sea-Power on History*. In it he argued that Britain owed its worldwide empire to its navy. The US Navy, important in the American Civil War (1861–65), had been neglected. Mahan recommended the USA restore its navy, acquire overseas bases and build a canal through Central America for ships to pass from the Atlantic to the Pacific without going round South America. This would cut the journey from the Caribbean to California by three-quarters, saving 11,263 kilometres (7000 miles) and six weeks.

The location map shows where maps 1 and 2 are. The yellow shows US expansion 1867–1914. Areas too small to show clearly are underlined in yellow. Map 1 – Guam, Wake, Midway, the Hawaiian islands and Samoa. Map 2 – Panama canal, Puerto Rico, Guantanamo (Cuba).

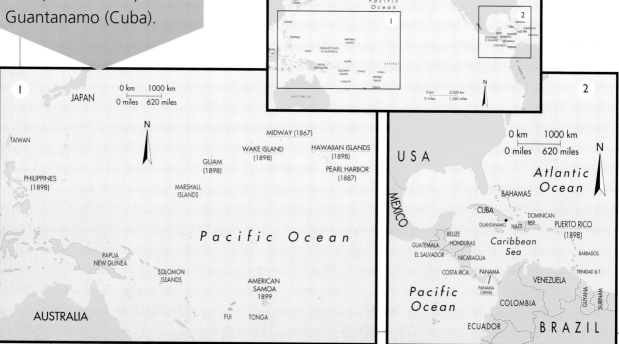

US cruisers destroy an outdated Spanish fleet at Manila Bay, in the Philippines in 1898.

A new power at sea

America listened to Mahan. By 1900 the US Navy had grown from twelfth to third largest in the world. America's naval power was shown in the Spanish–American war of 1898. At Manila Bay, Commodore Dewey's six modern ships sank ten outdated Spanish ships without losing a single man. Off Cuba, another US fleet lost just one sailor in destroying a second Spanish fleet. This war gave the USA control of the Philippines, Puerto Rico, the Pacific island of Guam and the right to build a naval base in Cuba. In 1898 the USA also took over Hawaii and in 1908 began building a naval base at Pearl Harbor. Between 1907 and 1909 the US Navy's 'Great White Fleet' of sixteen battleships sailed 73,600 kilometres (around 46,000 miles) round the world in a show of strength.

THE PANAMA CANAL

Building a canal through Panama started in 1882. It only succeeded after an environmental clean-up of swamps and undergrowth in 1904–06 wiped out mosquitoes carrying **yellow fever** and rats carrying **plague.** The US Corps of Army Engineers completed the 82 km-long canal between 1908 and 1914 for $380,000,000. Thanks to the canal the US Navy could switch its strength quickly to either the Pacific or Atlantic Ocean. Modern supercarriers are now too big to use it.

Pacific rivals

World War I...

As Britain's **ally** against Germany in World War I (1914–18), Japan used its navy to capture the German-controlled Shandong area of China and German **colonies** in the Pacific – the Mariana, Caroline and Marshall Islands. Japan kept control of the islands after the war ended in 1918. German U-boat sinkings of **neutral** American ships helped bring the USA into the war as Britain's **Allies** in 1917.

...and after

At the 1919 Paris Peace Conference, US President Woodrow Wilson launched the League of Nations, with the aim of settling disputes between countries peacefully. Unfortunately Wilson, a dying man, could not get America itself to join and this seriously weakened the League. The League also refused to adopt a declaration of racial equality suggested by Japan. The Japanese felt that, despite all their efforts to modernize their country, they were still not accepted as equals by Westerners.

The Prince of Wales with Japanese naval officers in 1921. The twenty-year-old Anglo-Japanese alliance ended that year. The US could now fight Japan without coming into conflict with Britain.

America and Japan

At the Washington Naval Conference, organized by the USA in 1921–1922, Japan was persuaded to agree that, for every five battleships America and Britain had, it would have only three. The US and Britain agreed not to strengthen bases west of Pearl Harbor, giving Japan superiority in its home waters. As part of the same agreement, the Anglo-Japanese alliance was dissolved after twenty years. This ended American fears that, in a war with Japan, the US might risk fighting Britain, too.

In 1924 Congress passed a law against Japanese **immigration** to the USA. The Japanese took this as a further insult by the West.

THE AIRCRAFT CARRIER

Carriers were pioneered during World War I. As they increased in size, ideas about possible uses for them changed. Japan's *Hosho* was the first purpose-built carrier actually launched (1922). The far larger USS *Lexington* and *Saratoga* and Japanese *Akagi* and *Kaga*, were all conversions made in 1927–28. In the 1930s America, Japan and Britain were the only nations to begin building large purpose-built carriers. The USS *Yorktown* carried 80 planes, the Japanese *Shokaku* 84, HMS *Illustrious* only 55 – but the British design was much better armoured and stronger.

Americans and Japanese thought carrier-borne planes in large numbers could cripple an enemy fleet at ranges far beyond those of a battleship's guns. World War II was to prove them right and make the battleship **obsolete**. Pearl Harbor was only one of the battles to show this.

The **USS** *Saratoga* was converted from a battle-cruiser that had been scrapped in accordance with the 1922 Washington Naval Agreement.

A world without work

Making jobs

The collapse of world trade between 1929 and 1931 caused mass unemployment in all the industrial nations. Japan was still recovering from a terrible earthquake which had wrecked Tokyo in 1923, killing over 100,000 people. In the USA conditions were made worse by droughts, which turned rich farmlands into 'dust bowls'. From 1933 onwards President Roosevelt's 'New Deal' programme tried to put Americans back to work by funding conservation projects and building dams. In Germany Adolf Hitler's Nazi government created jobs by building highways and re-arming for a future war.

Making trouble

Japan was poor in minerals, had no oil or rubber and, being very mountainous, had too many farmers for too little land. **Extremists**, especially in the army, favoured expanding the overseas empire by war. This would give Japan access to the raw materials it lacked, markets for its manufacturers and land on which to settle its growing population. Civilian politicians wanting continued co-operation with the West, rather than war, risked their lives. When Japan agreed to the London Naval **Treaty** (1930) putting new limits on naval building, Prime Minister Hamaguchi was **assassinated** at Tokyo railway station.

Yellow areas show Japanese expansion in the period 1894–1937. Islands that are too small to be seen are underlined in yellow.

MANCHURIA
(Japanese occupation 1931–2)
became
MANCHUKUO
(1932 Empire under Japanese protection)

MONGOLIA

JEHOL
(Annexed to Manchuria in 1937)

SAKHALIN
1905

CHINA

KOREA
1910

JAPAN
•Tokyo

Hiroshima

North
Pacific
Ocean

Nagasaki

•Shanghai

0 km   1000 km
0 miles   620 miles

N

TAIWAN
1895

MARIANAS

GUAM

MARSHALL ISLANDS

PHILIPPINES

PACIFIC ISLANDS
CAROLINE ISLANDS

Manchuria becomes Manchukuo

In 1931, without asking permission from the civilian government in Tokyo, Japanese generals ordered troops into the resource-rich Chinese province of Manchuria. In 1932 they set up a **puppet government**, pretending the area was an independent state, Manchukuo. When the League of Nations condemned the invasion of Manchuria as **aggression**, Japan withdrew from the League in 1933. In 1934 Puyi, China's last emperor and a Manchu, was made Emperor of Manchukuo. Real power, however, remained in Japanese hands. In 1937 Japanese troops in Manchukuo began a full-scale invasion of the rest of China.

Puyi, the top-hatted puppet ruler of Manchukuo, is surrounded by Japanese generals and officials.

THE 26 FEBRUARY 1936 INCIDENT

In 1936 junior army officers used 1400 troops to seize the Japanese parliament and prime minister's home. They assassinated two ministers and a general and demanded a new government. The rebellion was crushed in days and nineteen leaders were shot. But the army used the uprising to increase its power over government, arguing that this was the only way discontent among junior officers could be controlled. In 1938 a National **Mobilization** Bill geared business up for all-out war production, giving the government strict control over companies, unions, prices and the media.

Edging towards world war

War in China

By December 1937 Japanese troops had taken Beijing, Shanghai and Nanjing, where at least 150,000 civilians were massacred. Western eyewitnesses were horrified but helpless. When Japanese planes sank the US gunboat *Panay*, which was carrying Chinese **refugees** near Nanjing, Japan apologized and paid $2,000,000 compensation. America accepted this.

A Chinese baby screams amid the wreckage of a Shanghai railway station, bombed by the Japanese.

Although America accepted Japanese apologies for China, it wanted to stop Japan's aggression. But American opinion still favoured staying out of foreign wars and concentrating on getting people back to work after the **Great Depression**. Besides, Japan had an army of 2,000,000, while the USA had under 200,000.

Although, the Japanese naval tonnage was only 70 per cent of that of the US Navy, its carrier tonnage was equivalent to 94 per cent of the Americans'. If the USA was not yet prepared to re-arm for war there was little point in threatening one. A top-level secret **task-force** of Japanese bankers and military estimated that the US economy could produce ten times as much as Japan. But Japanese generals thought of America as a country famous for film stars, gangsters and jazz, not soldiers. America would continue to protest at the war in China, but do nothing.

Choosing an enemy

By 1938 the Japanese army thought the main aim should be to finish conquering China and confront the strong **Soviet** forces on the Manchukuo border. Japan's navy favoured driving south to control South-East Asia's oil, rubber and minerals, vital supplies for industry at home and war overseas. Expanding south, however, they risked war with the British, French, Dutch and Americans, who all had **colonies** or interests there.

Defeat and diplomacy

In 1938 and again in 1939 Japanese troops clashed with Soviet forces on the Manchukuo border, leading to large-scale fighting. Soviet armoured units and aircraft beat the Japanese repeatedly, killing over 17,000. This fighting showed the army it was not unbeatable and should concentrate on one war at a time. In September 1939 the Japanese asked for a ceasefire. The outbreak of war in Europe that month led the **USSR** to agree. In April 1941 the two countries agreed to remain **neutral** if the other went to war, thus saving both countries from the nightmare of a war on two major fronts.

Hard choices for America

Hoping for peace...

When Germany invaded Poland in September 1939 many Americans thought the USA should stay out of the European war. Opinion in the USA was strongly anti-German, just as it was anti-Japanese over Asia. But Americans thought Britain and France together would be able to resist Germany and that some sort of agreement about China could be **negotiated** with Japan.

...preparing for war

Germany crushed Poland in weeks, and in the spring of 1940 turned west to conquer Holland, Belgium and Luxembourg. France **surrendered** in June 1940. Britain **evacuated** its troops, abandoning their heavy equipment. American generals predicted Britain's early defeat.

Americans registered in their thousands for military service. These men are enlisting in the army. US pilots, trained in three months, were known as '90-day wonders'.

Japan seized the chance to take over France's **colonies** in South-East Asia. As the situation worsened in both Asia and Europe, American defence efforts expanded rapidly. In September 1940 – for the first time in its history – the USA ordered men to register for possible military service. By December 1941, US army and airforce manpower had risen to 1,600,000 and the number of navy vessels from 1100 to 1900.

American support

Roosevelt believed that, despite defeats, both Britain and China would continue resistance and that the USA would best serve its own security by supporting them without actually going to war.

Roosevelt pledged that America would be the '**arsenal** of **democracy**' – supplying the weapons Britain and its **allies** needed to defeat the dictatorships of Hitler (in Germany) and Mussolini (in Italy). This meant sending supplies to Britain and having the US Navy escort the ships carrying them, even at the risk of fighting German U-boats. In China it meant sending supplies and volunteer pilots. Meanwhile, more pressure was put on Japan by banning **exports** of petrol and scrap metal which Japan badly needed.

The Flying Tigers

The Flying Tigers were formed in April 1941 by Claire L. Chennault, a retired US Army Air Corps officer and training expert, who recruited 100 pilots and 200 ground crew to help China against invading Japanese forces. They trained at a British base in Burma and defended the Chinese city of Kunming and the 'Burma Road' supply route which carried supplies to Chinese troops. The Flying Tigers destroyed 286 Japanese aircraft for the loss of 50 US aircraft and nine pilots.

The Flying Tigers' proper name was the American Volunteer Group, but the origin of their nickname is obvious.

The great gamble

Planning for a knock-out

Faced with America's rapid arms build-up, Japanese leaders decided the USA meant war after all. They thought Japan's best chance of victory lay in destroying the US Pacific fleet at Pearl Harbor. They believed America would then be unable to interfere with the conquest of Asia for at least eighteen months. By then Japan's hold should be secure and even the USA would not be able to invade an entire continent across the world's biggest ocean.

If war was unavoidable, Japanese planners argued for starting before the USA became even stronger. While Japan negotiated in Washington, Admiral Yamamoto planned his surprise attack on Pearl Harbor.

Pearl Harbor – mistaking the dangers

American forces realized an enemy first strike was possible, but expected it would be at the Philippines, only 320 kilometres (200 miles) from Japanese-controlled Taiwan. In the remote Pacific island of Hawaii, where 150,000 local people – 37 per cent of the population – were of Japanese descent, the main fear was of **sabotage**.

An aerial view shows how Pearl Harbor's Battleship Row made an ideal target.

Looking the wrong way

Planes were therefore lined up close together to make it easier to guard them – but this also made them a much easier target from the air. Any attack on Hawaii was expected from the Japanese-controlled Marshall Islands, 3200 kilometres (2000 miles) to the south-west. No long-range air **reconnaissance** was ordered, and on the morning of Sunday, 7 December most guns were unmanned and without ready supplies of ammunition.

Swiftly, silently...

Yamamoto's plan depended on sailing six carriers and their support ships from Japan across 5500 kilometres (3400 miles) of the Pacific, without being spotted. Keeping radio silence – and shielded by bad weather – the Japanese **task-force** managed to sail within 450 kilometres (280 miles) of Pearl Harbor undetected and then launch its attack from the north.

A furious President Roosevelt asks Congress to declare war on Japan. The US did so on 8 December 1941.

A DIPLOMATIC DISASTER

Japanese **negotiations** continued in Washington to the very last. On Saturday 6 December there was a staff send-off party at the Japanese embassy. As a result of heavy drinking, only two senior staff were on duty next morning when the coded message came from Tokyo, carrying a formal declaration of war. Without junior staff, who were much faster at decoding and typing, the two officials failed to hand the declaration over to US officials until half an hour *after* the attack on Pearl Harbor had started, instead of 30 minutes *before*, as intended. America was predictably outraged.

Patriotism and production

PROVING A POINT

To prove their loyalty to the USA, thousands of Japanese-Americans volunteered. A Japanese-American unit, the 100th Battalion, composed largely of Japanese-Americans born in Hawaii, won so many medals for being wounded in action that it became known as 'the Purple Heart Battalion'. It later became part of the 442nd Regimental Combat team, which was the most decorated in US military history, winning four Distinguished Unit Citations in North Africa, France and Italy. In 225 days of combat the 10,000 men who served in it won 18,143 individual decorations.

Relocation

In 1941 there were 120,000 people of Japanese descent *(Nisei)*, two-thirds of them US citizens, living on America's west coast, where a Japanese invasion was thought most possible. Although there was little evidence to prove it, Japanese-Americans were suspected of disloyalty to their adopted country. So 112,000 *Nisei* were forced to leave their homes and businesses and live in ten camps far away from the coast, in inland states such as Arizona, Colorado, Wyoming and Arkansas.

Despite this treatment, over a thousand imprisoned *Nisei* volunteered to serve in the US armed forces. No Japanese-Americans were proved to have taken part in spying or **sabotage**. In 1944 the US Supreme Court ruled that relocation was **unconstitutional** and the camps were closed. Between 1948 and 1965 Japanese-Americans were paid $38,000,000 to cover their losses – less than a tenth of their value. Fewer than 10,000 Americans of German or Italian descent were relocated away from the west coast.

On the way to an unknown destination – relocated Japanese-Americans wait at a reception camp.

Collecting scrap rubber for the US war effort – rubber was one of the few key resources that the USA could not produce itself.

ARSENAL OF DEMOCRACY

Japanese planners guessed that America could produce ten times as much as Japan. They were wrong. In fact it produced even more. As America geared up for war, its vast natural resources and skilled labour force enabled it to feed and arm 12 million men and women, as well as helping it to support its **allies** overseas. In 1940 Roosevelt's promise to build 50,000 planes was met with amazement; by 1945 300,000 were built.

The United States Army Air Force had 2470 planes in 1939. By 1944 it had 79,908. In addition, US shipyards turned out 147 carriers and 215 submarines, as well as 952 other warships plus 5200 merchant ships and 88,000 landing craft. The US Navy expanded twenty-fold to become the biggest in the world.

The USA also produced two-thirds of the world's oil supplies. A tenth of all America's food production went abroad, mostly to the **USSR** and to Britain, where it supplied the millions of US soldiers who would invade Europe.

Victory at sea

After inflicting huge damage on the US Pacific Fleet at Pearl Harbor, the Japanese captured many Pacific islands. They intended to keep the **Allied Powers** at arm's length, to prevent the bombing of Japan and any interference in their Asian conquests. As America and its allies fought to roll back Japanese advances, four great naval battles helped decide the war.

Battle of the Coral Sea, 4–8 May 1942

This was the first battle in history when opposing fleets never saw each other, both relying on carrier-based planes as their main weapon. Japan aimed to take Port Moresby, New Guinea, as the base for invading Australia. Because Allied code-breakers could read Japan's naval orders, the US Navy knew the Japanese plans. The USA suffered heavier losses, but Port Moresby was saved.

Major carrier battles of the Pacific war 1942–44.

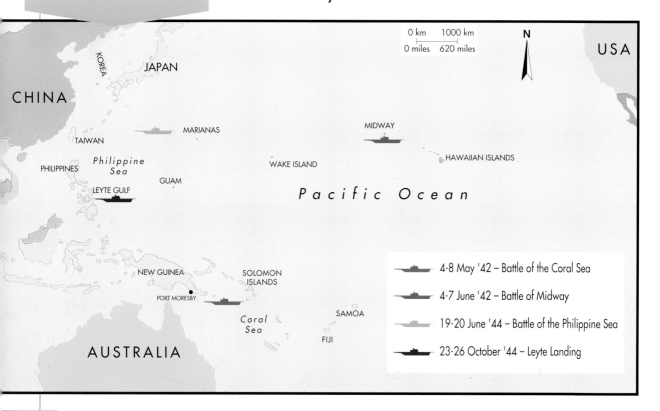

0 km 1000 km	
0 miles 620 miles	

N

USA

KOREA

JAPAN

CHINA

MARIANAS

MIDWAY

TAIWAN

Philippine Sea

WAKE ISLAND

HAWAIIAN ISLANDS

PHILIPPINES

GUAM

LEYTE GULF

Pacific Ocean

NEW GUINEA

SOLOMON ISLANDS

PORT MORESBY

SAMOA

Coral Sea

FIJI

AUSTRALIA

- 4-8 May '42 – Battle of the Coral Sea
- 4-7 June '42 – Battle of Midway
- 19-20 June '44 – Battle of the Philippine Sea
- 23-26 October '44 – Leyte Landing

Battle of Midway,
4–7 June 1942

The Japanese sent 145 ships to take Midway island, hoping to force the Americans to defend it. From Midway they intended to take Hawaii. The Americans once again decoded Japanese messages, so US Admiral Nimitz could plan accordingly. The Japanese lost four aircraft carriers, a blow from which they never recovered. From Midway onwards they could no longer attack, only defend.

Battle of the Philippine
Sea, 19–20 June 1944

The largest carrier battle of the war was fought while US troops were fighting for the Mariana islands. Japan could be bombed from there. Against a much stronger American fleet the Japanese lost 3 more carriers, 17 submarines and almost 400 planes – over 90 per cent of their remaining carrier-based aircraft.

Battle of Leyte Gulf,
23–26 October 1944

Japan's attempt to prevent US forces from recapturing the Philippines led to the biggest naval battle in history. The Japanese plan nearly worked – because they had changed their code so the US commanders had no advance knowledge. Both fleets blundered around, with the Japanese losing four more carriers during the battle and failing to prevent the US landings.

A *kamikaze* attack – most *kamikaze* planes were destroyed well before hitting their targets.

KAMIKAZE

In 1281 and 1284 the Mongol rulers of China sent huge fleets to invade Japan, but they were destroyed by typhoons which the Japanese called '*kamikaze*' (divine wind). As the war turned disastrously against Japan in 1944, suicide squads were formed to crash their planes on invading ships. Known as *kamikaze* pilots, they sank an American escort carrier at Leyte. When American forces invaded Okinawa, 2000 *kamikaze* pilots sank 36 ships and damaged 368 more. By the war's end some 5000 *kamikaze* had died.

America's Japan

America advances

US forces by-passed the islands where Japanese forces were strongest. As Japan lost its naval power these islands could no longer be reinforced or supplied. The first Japanese-held island to be taken, between August 1942 and February 1943, was Guadalcanal in the Solomon islands. The Japanese managed to **evacuate** 13,000 troops, abandoning their sick and wounded. Guadalcanal cost around 1700 US lives and at least 17,000 Japanese lives. In June 1944 US forces took Saipan in the Marianas, from where they could bomb Japan itself. The Americans planned to take Saipan in three days. It took three weeks.

Paying the price

In February 1945, after 72 days of bombing, 110,000 Americans landed to take Iwo Jima, an island half-way between Saipan and Japan. They planned to take the island in 14 days – it took 36. Japanese commanders knew they could not win the war but hoped high losses would make the **Allies** negotiate for peace, rather than demand Japan's complete **surrender**. On Okinawa the 172,000 US troops suffered 50,000 casualties. The Japanese lost 110,000 soldiers, plus 150,000 civilians.

Lt. General Richard K. Sutherland (left) accepts Japan's surrender, aboard USS *Missouri*, 2 September 1945.

The end – destruction

In March 1945 US bombers killed 100,000 civilians in a three-day raid on Tokyo. By May 13,000,000 Japanese were homeless. In August the dropping of atomic bombs on Hiroshima and Nagasaki and the **USSR**'s invasion of Manchukuo finally forced Japan to surrender.

A new beginning – democracy

For the first time in its history Japan was invaded by foreign forces. Under Allied **occupation** Japan adopted a **democratic** constitution which guaranteed citizens' rights and gave women the vote. Land was given to peasant farmers. Independent **trade unions**, mass media and political parties were allowed. Education was reformed.

Japan's democracy is now more than half a century old. Here, politicians try to catch the voters' interest on the streets at the 1993 elections.

THE POPULAR CONQUEROR

General Douglas MacArthur (1880–1964) graduated from West Point military academy with the highest ever marks. In 1905 he went to Tokyo as assistant to his father, a general. Douglas MacArthur ended World War I as a general himself, with thirteen decorations for bravery. In the 1930s he organized the Philippine army. In 1942 he lost the Philippines to the Japanese but reconquered the islands in 1945. As Supreme Commander of the **Allied Powers**, MacArthur took charge of the occupation of Japan. A strong supporter of democratic reforms, he became very popular with the Japanese. In 1950 he became Commander-in-Chief of UN forces against **communist aggression** in Korea and organized a daring and successful landing behind enemy lines. When he called for the bombing of communist China, President Truman dismissed him for trying to interfere in a political – rather than military – decision.

Japan's Japan

Wealth...

The **occupation** of Japan ended in 1952. Some US troops remained because Japan and the USA had become **allies.** The new constitution drawn up by the **Allied Powers** for Japan only allowed small forces for self-defence, so it could spend more on building new industries. In 1958 Japan launched the world's largest oil-tanker. By 1964 Japan was wealthy enough to host the Olympics and start the world's first 'bullet-train' service. Japan became the world's biggest producer of ships, cars, cameras, radios and TV sets.

The 200-kph (124 mph) bullet train is a symbol of Japan's post-war revival.

Then Japan switched away from heavy goods, such as steel and chemicals, which caused pollution and needed large imports of energy and raw materials – which Japan has never had. Instead, Japan used its highly-educated workers to make computers, photocopiers and other advanced, 'light' goods. By 1990 Japan had seven times as many industrial robots as the USA, and the world's largest merchant fleet.

...and health

The Japanese became not only richer than ever before but healthier, too. Life expectancy in Japan is now 77 for men, 83 for women, compared with 73 and 80 in the USA. The USA has more doctors per person than Japan but spends just over one and a half times as much on health as on defence. Japan spends almost five times as much on health as on defence.

Japan in the world

Japan has remained a close ally of the USA, and joined the United Nations in 1956. By 1989 Japan was second only to the USA in giving aid to poor countries and paying for the United Nations.

In the 1970s Japanese companies began building factories in South-East Asia, Europe and North America. By 1992 Japan had invested $386 billion abroad, almost half of it in the USA. The number of Japanese working or studying abroad had grown to 680,000.

Japan became an economic superpower but had neither the will nor the means to use military power abroad. During the 1990–1 Gulf War between the USA and its allies and Saddam Hussein's Iraq, Japan took no part in the fighting but paid $13 billion towards its costs. Japan also gave $110 million to help Kurdish **refugees** from the war and sent pollution experts to help clean up damaged oilfields afterwards. In 1992 Japan changed its laws to allow up to 2000 troops to serve abroad on peaceful UN missions.

Diggers made at the Komatsu factory in north-east England, an area which has the largest concentration of Japanese investment in Europe.

USA – the world's policeman?

A change of outlook

After World War I the USA had little interest in foreign affairs. In the 1920s prosperity at home was more absorbing than problems overseas. In the 1930s problems at home with unemployment and farming seemed more urgent than threats from abroad. The shock of Pearl Harbor was the price America paid for ignoring the rest of the world.

After World War II the USA was concerned at the **communist** take-over of Eastern Europe and, in 1949, China. As a result the USA and Britain took the lead in founding the United Nations as a more effective version of the League of Nations. The USA also funded the Marshall Plan to loan European countries – including defeated Germany and Italy – the money to re-build and begin trading again. In 1949 the USA founded the North Atlantic Treaty Organization (NATO) to defend the western democracies against the **USSR** and its allies.

This world map shows the locations of some US military actions since 1945. These are shown in yellow, with the date of the action.

CANADA

USA

North Atlantic Ocean

CUBA
DOMINICAN REPUBLIC 1965
HAITI 1994
GRENADA 1983
PANAMA 1989

N

SOUTH AMERICA

South Atlantic Ocean

UNITED-KINGDOM
BERLIN 1948

EUROPE

KOSSOVO 1999
LEBANON 1958 & 1983
LIBYA 1986
KUWAIT 1991
SUDAN 1998
SOMALIA 1992–94

AFRICA

RUSSIA

CHINA

KOREA 1950–53

INDIA

VIETNAM 1965–73

Indian Ocean

AUSTRALIA

0 km   2,000 km
0 miles   1,240 miles

Against communism and national aggression

Between 1945 and the break-up of the USSR after 1991, American foreign policy was based on stopping the spread of **communism**, which the USA believed aimed at taking over governments wherever possible. For this reason the USA sent armed forces to fight in Korea (1950–53) and Vietnam (1964–73). In 1991 the USA also led international forces to free Kuwait after it was invaded by Iraq. In 1999 the USA led the bombing campaign which drove Serb forces out of Kosovo because they were attacking local Albanian civilians.

Troops around the world

Fifty years after the end of World War II the United States still had 200,000 troops stationed around the world, to support its **allies** or take action in local trouble spots. In 1997, the largest number were in Germany (63,377) followed by Japan (37,137), South Korea (37,213), Britain (11,562), Italy (12,192), Panama (6,101), Spain (2,348), Turkey (3,056) and Bosnia (7,906).

RIVALS NO MORE

The US Navy is still the world's largest, consisting of 480,000 personnel, 13 aircraft-carriers, 102 submarines, 34 cruisers, 41 destroyers, 51 frigates, 1675 combat aircraft and 390 helicopters. Today's US carriers are far larger than those used in World War II. Nuclear-powered USS *Nimitz*, the world's largest warship, is 94,990 tonnes and carries 90 aircraft and 5700 crew.

Japan's Maritime Self-Defence Force is limited to home waters and consists of 43,100 personnel, 15 submarines, 62 destroyers and frigates, 110 aircraft and 100 armed helicopters.

The USS *Carl Vinson* underway. The US Navy has six aircraft carriers of the *Nimitz* class.

Time-line

1543		First Europeans land in Japan
1639		Japan cuts off foreign trade
1853		USA forces Japan to re-open foreign trade
1868		Japan's new government begins modernizing reforms
1890		A. T. Mahan publishes *The Influence of Sea-Power on History*
1894–5		Japan defeats China and takes over Taiwan
1902		Anglo-Japanese alliance
1905		Japan defeats Russia
1904–14		Panama Canal built
1910		Japan takes over Korea
1914–18		World War I
1917		USA enters World War I
1919		League of Nations founded at Paris Peace Conference
1922		Washington Naval Conference limits naval building
1924		USA bans immigration by Japanese
1929		World trade collapses
1930		London Naval treaty limits naval building
1931		Japan takes over Manchuria
1932		Manchukuo established
1933		Japan leaves the League of Nations
1937		Japan attempts to conquer all China
1939		Outbreak of World War II in Europe
1940		Japan takes over French colonies in South-East Asia
1941	7 December	Japan attacks US naval base at Pearl Harbor, Hawaii
1942	February	Japan captures Singapore, Britain's main military base in East Asia
	4-8 May	Battle of the Coral Sea
	4-7 June	Japanese navy defeated at Battle of Midway
1943	February	USA takes Guadalcanal
1944	19-20 June	Battle of the Philippine Sea, Saipan taken
	23-26 October	Battle of Leyte Gulf
1945	March	US bombers devastate Tokyo
	April	USA forces invade Okinawa
	6 August	Atom bomb dropped on Hiroshima
	8 August	USSR declares war on Japan
	9 August	Atom bomb dropped on Nagasaki
	14 August	Japan surrenders
	28 August	US troops land in Japan
1946		Japan adopts a democratic constitution
1949		North Atlantic Treaty Organization founded
1950–53		Korean War
1951		Peace treaty signed between Japan and USA
1964		Japan hosts Olympic Games
1970		Japan installs first industrial robots
1989		Death of Emperor Hirohito
1998		Japan hosts Winter Olympic Games in Nagono

Glossary

aggression	unprovoked attack
alliance	partnership of friendly nations
Allied Powers	countries fighting together against Germany, Italy and Japan in World War II, also known as the Allies
ally	a nation or state that is friendly to another nation
arsenal	place for storing or making weapons
assassinate	murder, usually for a political reason
attaché	literally 'attached', a diplomat with special expert knowledge
casualties	people killed or wounded
colony	land ruled by a foreign government
communism	government based on the idea that one ruling political party can run a country better than if ordinary people make their own decisions and keep private homes and businesses
communist	follower of communism
democracy	system of government based on the equal right of all citizens to choose and change their leaders freely
diplomacy	relations between nations conducted by peaceful means
empire	group of countries ruled by another
evacuated	taken to safety
extremist	someone with such strong views they are not prepared to give way at all
Great Depression	period after the financial panic and collapse of world trade in 1929; the worst was over by 1933
immigration	movement of people into a country
infamy	evil reputation
mobilization	organization of people or resources for war
Nazi	National Socialists Workers Party in Hitler's Germany
negotiations	settle a problem or dispute by talking and compromise
neutral	on nobody's side
obsolete	completely out of date
occupation	rule by a foreign army
plague	disease carried by fleas, often on rats, and often fatal
puppet government	a government which makes no real decisions but is ruled by another authority
reconnaissance	survey of an area to locate the enemy, or strategic features
refugees	people forced to move from their normal home
sabotage	deliberate damage to stop something working properly
Soviet	belonging to the Soviet Union
surrender	give in, admit defeat
task-force	armed force organized for a particular operation
tonnage	weight, rather than number, of ships in a fleet
trade union	organization to protect rights and interests of workers
treachery	betrayal by deception
treaty	official agreement between different countries
unconstitutional	against the laws protecting basic rights
USSR	Union of Soviet Socialist Republics; an empire in which communist Russia controlled neighbouring countries from 1917 to 1991; also known as the Soviet Union
yellow fever	acute tropical disease, which attacks the liver, heart and kidneys, often fatal.

Index